cure
the fear

Readers Respond to Cure the Fear:

--"I liked the lack of pressure, the step by step format, and the fact that you repeatedly tell me that it is easy and I can do it. (All of which is true.) It did help cure my fear of homeschooling high school. (I have read other books on this topic which have increased my fear and made me feel completely incapable of homeschooling high school.)"

--"After I read Cure the Fear of Homeschooling High School I was definitely more at ease. It really helped me get organized and understand what courses my daughter actually needed to graduate and attend the college/University she is interested in."

--"This was a very helpful book for a mom who has never homeschooled and was making the first go at it with my daughter who was a sophomore. Thanks for making this available; it was very helpful."

--"This book is the resource I desperately needed when I began homeschooling high school. Ann simplifies the planning process with step-by-step directions, printable worksheets, and plenty of encouragement along the way."

--"Even after reading several books about the final stretch and creating a basic plan for the upcoming high school years, I was surprised to learn so many new nuggets from Cure the Fear."

--"Not only did it answer all the questions I had — plus a few I didn't."

--"Ann's book was exactly what I needed to feel not just "okay" but to know that I had a plan in place. Her approach is very practical and very hands-on. She sends you right to pertinent resources and provides you with just the tools you need to organize and compare what you find. She takes you from big-picture long-term goals and drills right down to the details."

--"Not only does Ann ease parents' fears with her conversational style, but she also takes them by the hand and leads them through the process step-by-step."

--"Before I found Cure the Fear of Homeschooling High School, I felt intimidated and disorganized. After reading it, I felt equipped. I liked its no-nonsense yet friendly tone."

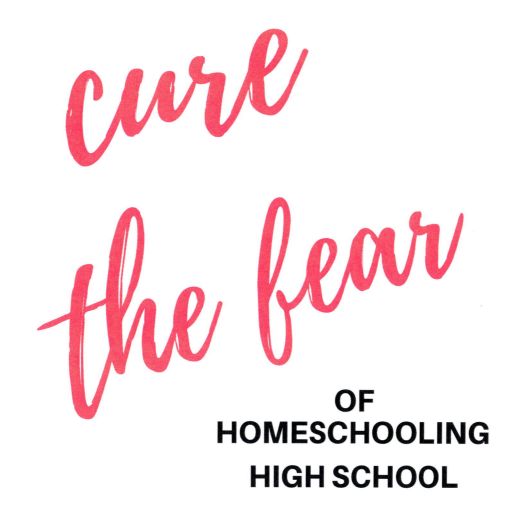

cure the fear

OF HOMESCHOOLING HIGH SCHOOL

HOW TO BE SURE YOU'RE NOT MISSING ANYTHING

A *step-by-step* HANDBOOK

BY

ANN KARAKO

"A goal without a plan is just a wish."

— *Antoine de Saint-Exupéry*

Table of Contents

"Give me six hours to chop down a tree and I will spend the first four sharpening the axe."

— Abraham Lincoln

Easing Your Fears

Why have you purchased this book?

No wait, let me guess.

Are you scared out of your wits about homeschooling high school?

Are you afraid you will make a big mess of it and ruin your kid's life?

I bet that's true for many of you that are reading these words. I know because I've been there myself, lol. Homeschooling high school is a scary proposition when you are looking at it from the front end.

For the first time in our homeschool career, we are thinking of having lessons in our home that go deeper than our own knowledge and/or ability. We are afraid we will not have the necessary expertise to handle the subject matter that our child will be dealing with. We are afraid we will mess up the planning process, and our child will not have enough credits to graduate. We are afraid our child won't get into college because we didn't give them the right courses. We wonder if our child will be sufficiently prepared to succeed in college after they have somehow been miraculously accepted. Or we are afraid they will be too stupid to hold down a job, because we didn't do it right.

And those feelings are not helped any by the huge amount of information out there that is just plain daunting. Many supposed "experts" make it appear that if my child hasn't read all these 500 books or volunteered for umpteen service organizations or learned how to write a 20-page research paper, they will never be qualified to graduate from high school or be accepted to college.

Or if I don't provide them the opportunity to take dual credit or AP courses, while simultaneously conversing with them in Russian and taking them to every museum in the tri-state area, I am a failure as a homeschool mom.

I get so frustrated reading that stuff, because I know it does not have to be that way. Homeschooling high school does not have to be difficult or scary. It can be easy, pleasing – even fun. But it's no wonder so many homeschooling families put their kids into public or private school once they hit ninth grade. If I believed even half of what those "experts" say, I would, too.

If you are admitting to yourself that you have read some of those things and have felt overwhelmed, then this book is a good fit for you. I am going to share what I've learned from my experience of homeschooling four of our five children all the way through high school. (The fifth was our little surprise, lol -- she starts ninth grade next year.) I want to help ease your fears and distill some of what you've heard down to a more manageable level.

To be specific, I'm going to share with you the process I used to prepare MYSELF for homeschooling high school, to educate myself about what is REALLY necessary. You'll be able to find out for yourself what you truly need to do and what is just not that important.

Then I'm going to walk you step-by-step through the process of planning curriculum for your teen. This task that seems scary now, and you worry you'll do it wrong, is actually very doable -- and I'm going to show you how to accomplish it in the simplest way possible. By the end of this book, you'll have a plan for your child all the way through to graduation.

And you know what? Once you get that curriculum plan set, a lot of those worries and fears will go bye-bye. There's something about having it all down on paper -- especially when it's something you can be proud of, which is what you'll have by the end of this book -- that makes you feel like you can do it. You've got this thing! And "we can stand tall, and face it all together…" (I'm listening to "Skyfall" in my earbuds as I write this. But it works, doesn't it? LOL.)

Maybe you're not worried.

Maybe you see this as a challenge that can be overcome, and you're actually looking forward to it. You just want to make sure you've covered all the bases, and you've picked up this book to get someone else's take on how to make it all happen.

I do that all the time. I am definitely a researcher. When I have something new coming up, or a decision to make, I will check out all the angles and get several opinions from people I trust. If that's what you're using this book for, then I am honored. I think you'll find some great ideas and be encouraged. "Can you feel all the love?" (the song switched to One Republic. What can I say? :-))

At the very least, you'll be able to take advantage of all the forms I provide with this book. I think they will help you streamline the process of planning high school, even if you already basically know what you're doing.

Planning for high school is not complicated.

There are just a few things to keep in mind, and once you know what they are, you can relax and enjoy the ride. Because all too soon you'll be graduating this kid. And you'll be able to look back with pride at how you both got through.

A lot of this book deals with preparation for applying to college, but that doesn't mean it's not applicable to the teen that doesn't intend to go there. It will be helpful for you as the parent to still complete each step in order -- because you might be surprised by what you learn. You might realize that your kid would be a good fit for college after all, when you realize that they don't need to know rocket science or be capable of winning the National Spelling Bee in order to get in. But beyond that, it's just a good idea to have a plan -- and this book will help you develop one.

Let me give you a quick overview of the book.

I want you to see the big picture first, so you know where we're headed. Then in each succeeding chapter we'll take another step down the path of preparing for high school -- and by the end, you'll have a workable plan to take your kid from the start all the way through senior year. Woot!

First I will outline perhaps the most important step of the whole process. If you skip the entire remainder of this book, don't ignore Chapter 2! Doing what it says will boost your confidence and reassure you that you CAN do this high school thing -- and that you won't scar your teen for life!

In Chapter 3, I'll give you help and guidelines to create a set of graduation standards for your child.

Chapter 4 is where we'll put together a very general plan for which subjects will happen when. There will still be lots of blank spaces, but that's OK at this point!

Chapter 5 will be a discussion on choosing core curriculum. I'll share some general sequencing tips for each of the subject areas. Now we'll be filling in most of those blanks with some actual course names. Woot!

In Chapter 6 we'll discuss electives. They are probably the most fun part of the whole process! They are like the icing on the four-layer cake that we've created in previous chapters. Get it -- four layers, four years of high school? Right?

Then Chapter 7 is the place where it all gets put together -- at least for one year of the plan. It will be time to choose specific curriculum to fulfill the course requirements you've set. I'll give tips on how to find what will fit your family and your teen.

Then you might think we'd be done, but I still (as always) have a few things to say, even after the plan is fully fleshed out. You need to know what it really takes to prepare your child for the real world, whether that be college or the workplace. It's not just what is included in a curriculum plan -- there's more to it than that. Read Chapter 8 to find out what it is. I think you'll be pleasantly surprised.

Chapter 9 is the conclusion, but it is more than that. In there I'll give you your marching orders to move forward year by year.

So let's just get started, shall we? I really want to get going, because Chapter 2 is the meat of the whole thing, and you're going to feel so much better once you get through it. Turn the page and be prepared to "get 'er done"!

How to use this ebook:

This book was originally formatted as an ebook, with clickable links throughout the text. People kept asking for a hardcopy format, so here it is! But that means there is no way within the book to have instant gratification about going to the online resources I mention.

Instead, I've created a password-protected resource page on my blog. While you are reading the book, have this page open on your device: https://www.annieandeverything.com/resources-cure-fear-ebook/. (**Password: curethefear**). All clickable links from the original ebook will be listed there, as well as links to all of the other resources I mention.

To make it easy, **anything that can be found as a link on the resource page is printed in** green. When you see green text, go look on the resource page for a corresponding link. And then click on it, and voilà! ALMOST instant gratification, lol! Believe me, it's worth making the effort to do this. Otherwise, you may not fully understand what I am talking about. So, green = link on resource page. Got it?

Names of printable forms are in blue. They are placed individually at the end of the chapter that they are associated with and ALSO all together at the end of the book. That makes it easier to print them out all at once, if you so desire.

OK, let's get started!

Chapter Two

The Crucial Confidence-Boosting First Step

Didja ever have something hanging over your head that seemed SO SO SO intimidating, yet once you girded your loins and got started, it wasn't that bad after all? Well, you are about to experience that same thing in regards to home-schooling high school! We're going to take the first step, and once that's done, you'll see that this isn't as big a deal as you thought it was. By the end of this chapter, you will feel TONS better -- you'll see!

I want to remind you of what I said earlier: this chapter is probably the most important in this whole book.

If you don't do anything else that I talk about in here, DO THIS. This first step for planning your high schooler's curriculum is SO EASY and yet SO EFFECTIVE at reducing fears.

One of the big fears about homeschooling high school is doing something wrong when it comes to preparing your teen for college. Many are afraid -- and I was, too -- that they will miss an important requirement, and their kid will not be able to go to the college of their choice -- all because mom messed up.

Well, this fear is a simple one to put to rest. Really; it's an easy one, y'all. There is no magical formula; nor is there a huge list of must-do's, the thought of which bows us down with dread, wondering how we will ever accomplish them.

No, actually we can get the information we need about high school curriculum requirements for college acceptance by completing a very easy exercise that can be done online. In an hour or less you can increase your confidence level by about 1000%.

And it doesn't matter if your kid is not planning on going to college. Doing this activity is a good idea anyway, because a) your kid might decide to go later, and/or b) educating yourself is one of the best ways to put yourself on solid ground when it comes to planning. You'll feel more confident about what you choose to do (and not do) if you know the big picture. Trust me on this one.

So what is this wonderful activity, you ask?

Simply this: the best way to know what colleges expect is to just look it up.

Yep, the information is there for the taking. We can get it right from the horse's mouth; we don't have to take anyone else's word for it. All those people who say you "should" make a portfolio to show colleges or that you "should" have three science lab courses or that you "shouldn't" skip a year of math are not the ones you want to use as your primary sources. We can do better.

We can find out from the colleges themselves.

This is so obvious, isn't it? But so many people try to plan their teen's coursework without knowing what their kid TRULY needs. They work from hearsay or look at public high school grad requirements and get intimidated.

If we want to know what courses our kid needs to get into college, we just need to go to the colleges and ask them.

OK, well, we don't really need to ask them verbally. Because the fact is that every college/university has a website these days. And on that website is a section for admissions -- which includes admissions requirements, y'all.

And lookee there! Whatever the college wants is written down in black and white. It will say how many credits of high school English the college requires, how many credits of math, of history, etc. It will even sometimes list specific courses that the admissions department would like to see the applicant to have taken in high school, like American History or British Literature.

It is neither difficult nor time-consuming to pick several colleges and look this information up on their websites. Sometimes it won't be in the general admissions section; then you need to look for the catalog. Often you can use the search box and type "catalog." You might have to download a PDF. No biggie -- you may want to look it over later, anyway. College catalogs are a WEALTH of handy information.

But don't do this for only Harvard and Yale. Just sayin'. :-)

No, the most helpful thing to do is to look at a cross-section of colleges and universities that your child might be interested in attending. Look at the local community college, and then maybe a state school, a couple of private colleges, your own alma mater, and ok, even an Ivy League, IF that's where your child might be headed. (But don't overwhelm yourself by looking at one if this cannot be a reality for your child. You will just tempt yourself into thinking you "should" try to fulfill their requirements anyway. NO, no, no.)

I've created a screencast -- only available to readers of this book -- to show you how to look at the website and determine where the requirements are. There are a couple of tricks to it -- once you see them, you'll be able to do it for yourself much more easily.

Go to this link on the resource page to watch the screencast: Finding College Admissions Requirements Online

You don't have to do this exercise all in one day. But I would not be surprised if you end up doing so, just because it's so easy. Especially with my handy-dandy *College Requirements Cross-Section* chart for you to fill out. **Go to the end of the chapter and print out a couple of copies NOW.** Pick out a few colleges (at least three or four) of varying levels and enter their requirements into the chart. (You'll need at least two copies of the form, because there is only room for the data from two colleges on each copy.)

As you work, you're going to see some amazing and very reassuring things.

The first one is that all colleges have different requirements. Let me repeat that: each and every college/university has its own requirements for what it expects to see from its app-licants. There are no state laws about this, because every school draws students from many different states of the union. Schools know that a child from one state may have been required to have so many credits of history in high school, but a child from another state may not have been required to have that many. So the colleges determine their own requirements, which may or may not match those of the state they are in.

For example, Penn State University gets applicants from all over the country. If they required everyone to have fulfilled the state of Pennsylvania's public high school graduation requirements in order to apply, they'd be turning a lot of students away -- and losing revenue, hello.

So Penn State has determined their own individual applicant requirements. These are much more broad and much less strict than those governing the state of Pennsylvania's public school system. This way someone from Ohio, who hasn't taken Pennsylvania state history, which is a requirement to graduate from public school in the state of Pennsylvania, can still apply. See what I mean?

So why does this matter?

Well, it is in fact VERY freeing!! Once you understand that admissions requirements vary from one college to the next, then you begin to realize that there is no one right way to do this high school thing. You don't have to try to do it the way someone else does it!! You can be you! Your kid can be your kid! You discover how flexible a high school curriculum can be -- and then the task becomes a whole lot easier.

Another interesting thing to notice, too, is that many colleges do not require very many credits at all. This can also be very relieving. Not in the sense that we can ditch the rest of high school and only do the ones the college requires, because I would not recommend that at all. BUT, it does remind us of one of the great perks of homeschooling -- the fact that we are in charge. We can decide how many credits our child needs to graduate and what courses he is required to take.

We do need to follow the homeschool laws in our state (more on that later in the book), but our curriculum plan for our child can be one that we design without being afraid of completing college requirements -- because they really are so few in comparison to a full high school curriculum. We fit them in, and then for the rest we have pretty much free rein! How fun is that?

Of course, most 8th-grade and younger students do not know where they want to go to college, so if you are a mom who is just starting to think about high school, right now this is just a data-gathering exercise. If you do happen to know that your child WILL be going to XYZ College, then by all means look up those requirements and plan that child's high school curriculum to meet them.

If you have already started homeschooling high school with your teen and have not done this exercise, then DO NOT DELAY. Because chances are you are swimming in a fog of uncertainty, basing your curriculum plan on hearsay or what you remember from your own high school. And you don't have to live like that.

Take an hour and find out for yourself, from the actual places that determine these things, what your child NEEDS to do to be ready to apply for college. Not what someone else says might be good, but what the colleges themselves say they really must have. You will be VERY glad you did!

Even if your child is still unsure of their college/career goals (and they might not figure that out for awhile, just sayin'), it is extremely helpful to get an idea of what will generally be required by most colleges and what your child needs to do to meet those requirements. Because from this information you can make an overall plan of classes that will fulfill the requirements for most places. Which is exactly what we will do over the course of this book.

I believe doing this little bit of research will ease some of the fear about homeschooling high school. When we know what colleges expect, we can plan to achieve that. It is not something we need to go into blind. Colleges do not have some magical hidden process by which they decide on the fitness of their applicants. It's all there in black and white, written on their websites and/or in their catalogs.

Don't skip this step, y'all.

And don't think that reading this chapter is enough to give you the knowledge and the confidence. Later on you won't remember what you read here, and you'll start to let those fears take over again. Trust me on this one!

Print out the chart, check out some college websites, and fill it in as you go. Then keep it handy. The act of actually doing this will ease that place inside you that is scared of not doing enough. You'll be able to look at exactly what you found out whenever you need to. You'll remember the feeling of relief as you noticed that everything I've said is true. You'll be empowered. And all of a sudden this homeschool high school thing won't seem as intimidating anymore.

--Hey, I just had a thought. If you're a parent who KNOWS WITHOUT A SHADOW OF A DOUBT that your kid isn't going to college, then you could spend some time looking up the requirements of several different career paths. Maybe your daughter wants to become a beautician -- then check out the requirements to get into beauty school. Your son is thinking about welding -- look up what is necessary to get accepted to be trained. If the child has no specific aspirations yet, then research a selection of careers, from dental hygienist to retail or service employee to x-ray tech or others.

Though I've not done this particular exercise myself, I'm betting that knowledge of what is expected to be accomplished before someone enters these college-alternative programs will empower you and give you confidence as you proceed with planning high school.

AFTER you have filled out the chart -- and only then -- move on to the next chapter.

There we're going to talk about designing your child's graduation requirements. Again, this won't be as bad as you fear. Especially now that you know how easy it will be to fulfill what the colleges want!

College Requirements Cross-section

	College #1	College #2
Name of School		
Math		
Number of Credits		
Specific Required Courses		
Unacceptable Courses		
English/Language Arts		
Number of Credits		
Specific Required Courses		
Unacceptable Courses		
History/Social Studies		
Number of Credits		
Specific Required Courses		
Unacceptable Courses		
Science		
Number of Credits		
Number of Lab Courses		
Specific Required Courses		
Unacceptable Courses		
Fine Arts		
Number of Credits		
Specific Required Courses		
Unacceptable Courses		
Foreign Language		
Number of Credits		
Specific Required Courses		
Unacceptable Courses		
Electives		
Number of Credits		
Specific Required Courses		
Unacceptable Courses		

Chapter Three

What Should YOU Require?

Are you feeling better already?? You should be. One look at that chart you made of college admissions requirements should be enough to get you into your happy place pretty easily. And it wasn't even that hard to fill out, was it?

This next step in planning your child's high school curriculum will be little more difficult. Not in the sense of the actual process, but in the amount of thinking and discussing you'll have to do to get it accomplished. But this is all good stuff, I promise. Again, it helps boost your confidence in what you've determined for your teen. You can look back at your decision-making process and know that it was solid.

The next step is looking at the big picture of what you think makes a good high school education -- i.e., developing a set of graduation requirements for your child.

Determining your homeschool's graduation requirements means you will always know where you're going and what you need to do to get there. Trust me, having a big-picture plan is going to be EXTREMELY helpful to keep you from worrying while you homeschool through the high school years!

And the ideal time to do this is BEFORE your child starts 9th grade. Maybe even while they are in late elementary or early middle school. This way we can think it all through and make decisions without pressure. We want to have clear thoughts as we decide what we want our teen to know before entering the adult world, whether that be college or the workplace. So feel free to take as much time as necessary with this step. No rush here.

If your teen is already in high school, no worries.

You can and should still complete this step. As you set your requirements, you can take into account what they've already done. But it's important to spend time thinking about what YOU think makes up a good high school education, so that you can make the changes necessary to bring it about for your child. After you're done with this step, you'll no longer feel like you're flying blind. You'll have a big-picture plan -- and you can start figuring out how to work it.

You may find that one time doing this step will suffice for all your kids, or you might end up doing it anew for each student. My #1 and #2 are so different that I needed to almost entirely revamp what I had done for the first to better fit the second… and that's OK. Let me just revisit a huge point from the first chapter that is important to keep in mind: there is no one right way to do this high school thing! (Exclamation point!!) If you remember that, it all seems less overwhelming.

So here's what you need to figure out: based on what you've seen in the college catalogs and what your child's goals are after high school, how many credits of each subject will you require for graduation? Will you require four full years of math, or can your child just take three? Do they need foreign language credits, and if so, how many? Do they need to take American History, specifically? Or Government? Or a science lab? How many credits will you require in total?

Here again, a little education of ourselves goes a long way towards boosting our confidence.

There are two crucial pieces of research to do that will each in its own way provide information that will ease your fears and help you along the path of deciding what is best for YOUR homeschool.

1 This first one may seem crazy at first, but humor me, ok? The first piece of research to do is to check out many different states' PUBLIC high school graduation requirements. I know, I know; we are homeschoolers, and we don't do what the public schools do. I am all about that.

BUT for some reason, as we begin to think about homeschooling high school, it is common to think that all the sudden we need to worry about public high school requirements. I did it, too! "High school is different," we say. "My child's future is at stake." "I want to make sure he is competitive with the public high schoolers when it comes to being considered for college acceptance." Etc. etc.

So how to address those issues? Do the research. This is another one NOT to skip. It was a huge eye-opener for me, and there is no substitute for seeing it with your own eyes.

The easiest way (and the best one, as you'll see in a moment) to check public high school graduation requirements is to look at a chart with ALL the states. Don't narrow your view to your local school district; that's a recipe for anxiety. Instead, look at the big picture.

There is a handy chart (and it's fairly recent, from 2013) that we can study. Go to the resource page to view the chart.

Find this link:
Chart of Public School
Graduation Requirements
for all 50 States

(BTW, It's helpful to know here that in high school terms, **a credit is a course that lasts a full year, and ½ credit is a course that lasts only a semester**. We'll obviously get more into detail on that later in the book, but for now you need to know this in order to fully understand the chart.)

As you look at that chart, what jumps out at you? Do you notice the VAST difference in the total number of credits needed to graduate for the different states (shown in the first column)??? Crazy, isn't it? The range is from 13 to 24 -- that's a BIG range!

Do you also notice that each state differs in how many credits of core subjects they require, and how many credits can be "other"? Take a look at that, if you haven't already.

What do these differences between states mean for you?

It means that you have LOTSA LEEWAY in determining the number of credits -- and the courses they represent -- that your kids have to complete in order to graduate from your own homeschool. If the individual states can vary so widely in their public school requirements, then we don't have to feel bound to follow any one of them in particular.

Also, we can extrapolate from the chart we completed in the previous chapter that colleges do not look at the total number of credits that your kid has accomplished; they just look to see if certain specific course requirements have been met. They have people applying to them from all over the states and abroad -- they can't be that picky about the total number, or they would have to refuse a good portion of their applicants.

(And there were collective sighs of relief heard 'round the country...)

When it comes to specific courses, our students don't HAVE to complete anything beyond what we found out about college requirements in Chapter Two. Again, the states don't even agree! So why should we feel that we have to do what our state does in the public schools?

Let me repeat: there is just no need for us to feel like we have to meet the number of credits the local school district requires -- or any other public school district, for that matter.

But wait!! Can we just ignore our state's laws altogether??

NO, that is NOT what I'm saying.

What I AM saying is that we can ignore our state's PUBLIC school laws. We DO need to be very familiar with our state's HOMESCHOOL laws, which is the second piece of research we need to do in order to plan our own graduation requirements.

2 It is VERY important that you research your state's law when it comes to HOMESCHOOL graduation. Let me put it even more bluntly: **it is FOOLISH if you do NOT know your state's homeschool laws when it comes to any aspect of homeschooling, and especially high school.** So if you haven't looked them up yet, GO THERE NOW. Do not pass go; do not collect $200 -- this is a MUST DO FOR EVERY HOMESCHOOLING MOM.

(And while I will be cutting to the chase and clueing you in on what I know about most states in just a minute, that does not negate your responsibility to look things up for yourself and verify what I say in regards to your own state. Just sayin'!!!)

You can do this by going to HSLDA.org or by doing a Google search for "Missouri homeschool law" (for example). Look for the law itself, not someone's interpretation of it. You'll find this at sites that end in .gov.

Do yourself a favor and PRINT IT OUT.

You will most likely want to refer back to it again and again, so save yourself time and effort and just make yourself a hard copy now. You can keep it with all of the forms from this book that you will fill out. Then whenever you doubt, or have a question, or need to make a change, it will be easily found.

I think it's a good idea to look at the law itself, rather than some blog's interpretation of it, because then you can be CONFIDENT in what you do. You're not taking anyone else's word for what the law says -- you have its own words right in front of you. Now, if it is difficult to understand, then by all means try to find more information. Most states have homeschool organizations that can explain the law to you if you are unsure. But always start with the law itself.

Every state is different; I can't adequately address each one's laws here. But there is one thing I can say with a fair amount of certainty:

MOST STATES DON'T HAVE ANY GRADUATION REQUIREMENTS FOR HOMESCHOOLERS.

Wait, what? you say. Repeat that, please? you ask.

Happy to oblige: Most states do not have ANY graduation requirements for homeschool students.

But why do I see graduation requirements listed on my state's education website? you demand.

Those are those silly PUBLIC SCHOOL graduation requirements that were summarized in the chart we just looked at. Those DO NOT apply to homeschoolers. You do NOT have to fulfill them.

Only a handful of states do have HOMESCHOOL graduation requirements. If your state homeschool law does not specifically say a child must complete x, y, & z to graduate, then your state probably doesn't have any!!

I took a poll in my Facebook group called It's Not that Hard to Homeschool High School. In that admittedly very informal poll, the only states reported to have homeschool graduation requirements are PA and NY. In CA, LA, and TN, it depends which path you take (and if you live in those states you should be aware of your options). In the VAST MAJORITY of states (although some were not accounted for), there were NO graduation requirements for homeschooled students. Nope. Zilch. Noodle!

Guess what? That means that for most of you out there, you can determine your own graduation requirements without fear.

YOU can decide how many credits of math, or how many of English, or history, or whether a foreign language is necessary, or if PE is something you want to mess with (I didn't, lol).

I do get that in some respects, it may seem intimidating to think about determining your own homeschool graduation requirements. But it is actually a wonderful thing. **Here are just a few of the benefits:**

💗 You can individualize the requirements to each child. You don't have to have the same set of requirements for all of your children. One might be required to do more math (maybe they are planning a technical major in college), or you might allow another to replace literature with philosophy, if that is their bent. Or you might have a special needs child, whose requirements need to be more closely tailored to their strengths or weaknesses.

💗 You can adapt your requirements to your family homeschool philosophy. If you are unschoolers, you might eschew the entire grading system and find a different way to assign credits. Or even "conventional" homeschoolers may prefer an emphasis on literature/living books or practical experience or whole language learning or scientific experimentation or whatever else.

You can outright MODIFY your graduation requirements as your circumstances or needs change. What you determine before your child enters high school may not reflect their needs by the time they hit junior year (or whenever). My one child hated math but loved languages. So somewhere in the middle of her high school years, we let go of a math credit and added more language credits to her "requirements." There are also life circumstances that get in the way -- maybe finances or an illness in the family mean you have to scale way back on what you thought you would require. It's all THOROUGHLY OK.

The key to remember is that since YOU decide all this -- based on your own SOLID research of the FACTS -- your child is not "missing something." No high school education is going to cover all the wisdom and knowledge of man, lol. What you deem important for your child to know is what your requirements will be. Let the rest go!!

Do NOT let the fear-mongers make you feel like you have to jump through a lot of hoops or your kid won't succeed or get into college.

Those are most often public school representatives, have you noticed that? Like the math teacher down the street, or the mom of your kid's childhood friend. It's usually people who have NO CLUE about homeschooling, but they think they have the right to voice their opinion, regard- less. Gotta love 'em -- but don't believe 'em.

Don't accept information (from any source other than your state's homeschool law) that tells you that you MUST have this, that, and the other thing in your child's course of study or on their transcript or even as their extra-curricular activities.

You don't HAVE to have anything beyond what the home-school law spells out.

It really gets me riled when I see misinformation disseminated around Pinterest and other social media. I very strenuously avoid the words "you must" or "your child must" for that very reason! (And if you see me using them that way, please call me on it!)

Sometimes well-meaning homeschoolers are just uninformed about the truth. Well, that doesn't need to be you any more. Fly, be free!! Bask in your right to determine your own home-school graduation requirements for your children (if you live in one of the MANY states that allows you to do so), now that you've done your research and feel confident in this reality.

But once you've revelled in that for a moment, next comes the question: So what do we do with this information? Well, it's time to sit down and think through what you want YOUR child to know before leaving their time of mandatory education that is high school.

Print out my *Graduation Requirements Planning* chart at the end of the chapter. Armed with your chart of college requirements from Chapter Two and your state's homeschool law, start playing with combinations of credits until you come up with a plan that meets what you think is best for your child.

(Underneath the squares with the usual subjects, you'll see some squares with white lines in them. Those are for you to fill in with any other specific requirements that you might want to include, such as work-study, health, PE, etc.)

This may take a few days as you think and discuss and think and discuss and think and discuss some more. And play with numbers in the chart. But it's actually a fun process. You can let your teen have input, if you like, or it can just be you and your spouse. I enjoyed hearing what my husband had to say about his desires for our kids and working with him to plan their education.

Right now this is just a list of numbers. We are not determining specific courses or where they will fit in chronologically. We are just determining the number of credits for each core subject and how many credits of electives to require.

One caution, though, is a reminder that based on our college requirements chart from Chapter Two, there is no NEED to have your teen do all of the core subjects EVERY year. I totally get that this may be a want of yours, and that is OK. But even the most academic kids need a break sometimes. And those that aren't academic DEFINITELY do, lol.

From my own experience, I found myself lightening the load as the years went on, because my kids became overwhelmed with all the heavy stuff. So I'm just suggesting that you consider this on the front end and perhaps allow for more electives, rather than every core subject every year. Just sayin'. :-)

Our next step will be to make a general plan. THAT is where we decide when these credits will happen. Once you've determined your graduation requirements, the general plan follows rather easily. Are you ready?

Don't go to the next chapter until you (and your spouse) have decided on a final list of credits your child needs in order to graduate. **One step follows from the next, and you will only undermine your confidence, rather than build it up, if you skip any.**

Graduation Requirements Planning

Directions: Fill out the column under Trial #1 first with possible numbers of required credits in each subject row.
Then try a new scenario in the Trial #2 column, and so on.

	Trial #1	Trial #2	Trial #3	Trial #4	Trial #5
English/Language Arts					
Math					
History/Social Studies					
Science					
Foreign Language					
Fine Arts					
Electives					
_____					
_____					
_____					
Total					

Chapter Four

The General Credits Plan

Woot!! Now we're getting somewhere! We've looked at what colleges require, and we've designed our own graduation requirements.

Now it's time to pull out our puzzle-solving skills.

We're going to take those graduation requirements and create a GENERAL plan for our teen. In other words, we're going to decide which subjects should happen when -- not specific courses yet, just overall subjects. It can take a little bit of trial and error as you fill in the spaces with numbers, but it's really not that difficult. (This is the shortest chapter in the book for a reason, lol.)

This is a good place to point out that high school credits don't all have to take place in grades 9 through 12. Sometimes your child might be ready for Algebra 1 in 8th grade, for example. I personally don't recommend doing a full load of high school courses in middle school, but sometimes you can get two or three credits out of the way.

I would limit this to core courses, though -- not electives. I don't really have any rationale for this other than my own notions about what it means to be "in high school," though. To me it's not just about content but about age. So in our family, my kids took Algebra, their first year of a foreign language, and Physical Science in 8th grade -- and that was all.

Your first task for this chapter is to print out the *General Credits Plan* at the back of the chapter. You might want to print multiple copies and try out a different scenario on each one. Or you could just use pencil and erase a lot, lol. Or you could cut up a bunch of sticky notes, one for each credit, and play with placing them in different boxes until you like what you see. Whatever floats your boat! :-)

Fill out the plan by placing your required credits into blocks on the form. If you decided that your child needs four years of English, then you will put a "1" in the English box under each year. If you think only three credits of Math are necessary, then you might choose to put a "1" in the Math row only under 9, 10, and 11.

You can decide to get the heavy coursework out of the way early, or you can decide to spread it out more. You can decide when they might need some elective credits, although there is no need here yet to specify what, unless it's obvious.

For example, my first was getting lots of violin credit, and I knew that from the beginning, so I was able to specify "violin" on one of the lines and the corresponding number of credits under each year. But #2 was gonna take several electives that we hadn't decided on yet, so I just used the word "elective" and put the numbers of elective credits where they needed to be.

As you work on the general plan, keep in mind that a core course is going to equate to about one lesson or one hour of work per school day -- and maybe a little less for an elective. One credit means one lesson/hour per day for the whole year; .5 credit means around one lesson/hour per day for a semester only. This is important because you want to be aware of how much time you are expecting your child to work on school every day. Plan for around 5-7 credits per year, and unless you want an overworked and frustrated teen, don't plan for the top end of that range for every year.

People do, you know. They talk about their kids taking seven or more credits EVERY. SINGLE. YEAR, as if it's perfectly reasonable and is actually expected by colleges. But you know better now, don't you?? Thanks to your research in Chapter Two, you know that this kind of overload is not necessary nor expected. So when you hear those types talking about it, you can be confident in your own factual knowledge, rather than being intimidated by their -- gonna say it -- ignorant claims. Woot!

So as you try to fit your graduation requirements in the plan, you might realize that they are actually too steep, so you might want to rework them a little to be more achievable; or you might realize that you need to beef them up a bit more. You might realize you can graduate your child early so he can go get a job for a semester before college; or you might decide he can look for an internship and count it as high school credit during a certain semester. The possibilities are endless!

Keep playing with combinations until you have a plan that looks workable and not too intimidating. Again, it's OK to set high goals; but don't set yourself up for failure before you begin by cramming the plan so full that you or your teen are afraid of how to accomplish it.

Please know, too, that the plan at the beginning and the actuality at the end might not (probably won't, actually) match each other. LOL! Circumstances change; plans that seemed great turn out to be not-so-great; the child who at one time loved math decides halfway through junior year that she absolutely cannot stand to take another course of it -- you get the idea. One of the beauties of homeschooling is that we can flex as needs change. I just love that, don't you?

But that doesn't mean we shouldn't plan.

All of these steps in preparing for high school are crucial, because they give us the confidence to do it. Completing each step in the process helps us feel empowered, even qualified, to think about graduating a homeschooled student down the road. Once you have a general plan in place, one that is based on YOUR OWN graduation requirements that YOU decided based on YOUR research about college requirements and your state's homeschool laws, the worst is over!

After this it's just a matter of deciding which specific courses to include each year -- we'll do that for core courses in the next chapter.

General Credits Plan

Directions: Write the number of credits for each subject in the box under the appropriate grade.

	Grade 8	Grade 9	Grade 10	Grade 11	Grade 12
English/Language Arts					
Math					
History/Social Studies					
Science					
Foreign Language					
Fine Arts					
Electives					
_____					
_____					
_____					
Total:					

Chapter Five

Planning Core Courses

By now you should be feeling like maybe homeschooling high school is not that hard (which is basically my mantra, lol). Because it really doesn't have to be. We tend to make it hard because we don't have enough information, and so we place unreasonable expectations on ourselves.

As we've found, the way to solve this problem is simply to educate ourselves -- but to do it in the right way. I'm gonna repeat myself, because I think this is SO important: don't pay attention to blog articles and websites that give you a long list of things you "must" do to homeschool high school correctly. There are very few "musts" when it comes to homeschooling high school!

You should already be feeling better in that regard. Some of those fears that you had before starting this book should already be subsiding, because now you've done the research and found out the truth for yourself, rather than listening to those people with the long "must" lists. Am I right? So let's keep moving onward and upward!

Now that we have a basic plan, we can start to fill in the specifics. In this chapter we'll deal with selecting core courses, and in the next chapter we'll work on electives.

By core courses I mean Math, Science, History/Social Studies, English, and Foreign Language. These are the subjects that almost every college (other than community colleges) will require from an applicant to one degree or another.

Determining the specifics for the core courses is a very simple process after you've done the work of creating your general plan. Usually there is a standard progression to follow, so filling in the blanks doesn't take much thought.

One caution regarding high school requirements.

I said this in an earlier chapter, but I'm going to say it again: We homeschoolers tend to be overachievers, and so we start off thinking our child is going to do all of the core courses every year of high school. I get that, I really do. I had very high expectations for homeschooling myself.

But as someone who has graduated three children from our homeschool -- and has another graduating next month as of this writing -- I would advise against that. It leads to a LOT of pressure. High school core courses take a lot of time each day to complete. And grades matter now. Not every student is best served by having to slave away all day on core courses.

And guess what? "Senioritis" is real, lol. That means your kid will most likely (unless mine were all just rebellious teenagers — and they weren't) have a very hard time being motivated to do school their senior year. So you might want to build more electives into that year, so that at least they will be studying subjects they enjoy.

It's not too late to go back and change your graduation requirements and/or your general credits plan. Just sayin'. :-)

OK, end of public service announcement. :-) Let's look at each core subject to learn the progression and how to choose which courses for your teen to take. Right now we are just naming courses; we are not finding exact curriculum. More on that later in the book.

Math

Math is one of those subjects that proceeds in a typical order for high school. The first high school credit given for math is Algebra 1, so that generally happens in 9th grade (although if your child is ready, it is possible to take it for credit in 8th grade). After that comes Geometry, then Algebra 2 (which also generally includes Trigonometry), Pre-Calculus, and finally, Calculus.

Recently there has been more talk about reversing the order of Geometry and Algebra 2, so that Algebra 2 comes right after Algebra 1. As a former math teacher, I can see merits in both sequences. Whichever you think is best will be fine.

But I want to remind you that not every child has to do all of these math courses. Only those who take Algebra 1 in 8th grade even have the possibility to get as far as Calculus, for instance. And as I mentioned earlier, many colleges only require three credits of math for their applicants -- so you might prefer to stop after Algebra 2, anyway. Consumer Math and Statistics are also options for math -- although you will want to be sure the college will accept them as high school math credits. If you've done your college requirements research, you will know that. :-)

If you haven't already done so, print out a copy of the *Planning*

Core Courses form at the end of this chapter. Using your *General Credits Plan* as a guide of where to put them, fill in the specific math courses your teen will take in the appropriate boxes.

Science

The first science course that is generally considered worthy of high school credit is Physical Science. After that the student can take Biology, then Chemistry, then Physics. The order of these is not set in stone, but often the difficulty level of the material, and the fact that each science course requires comprehension of a particular math level, means that this is the best sequence for most students.

Again, though, college requirements vary. If your child is not a budding scientist, doctor, or engineer, you may be better off not requiring all of these. There are also other possibilities for science courses out there, such as Astronomy or Marine Biology.

One thing to remember about science is that usually at least one lab course is required by colleges. It's a good idea to plan ahead for which one(s) that will be in your homeschool. In my family, we did Chemistry for our lab, because I had no interest in dissecting specimens in Biology, lol.

IN CASE YOU'RE GETTING FREAKED OUT ABOUT NOW: Cuz you're thinking about math and science, right? And how impossible it's going to be for you to teach them to your student??

Deep breaths; don't go there yet. Right now we are just

making a plan of courses. There are all sorts of options for how these courses happen. We WILL discuss this; I promise -- but not right now. ONE STEP AT A TIME.

So, moving on...

History

For history (or social studies, if you prefer), you might have found in your research that most colleges require only these courses: World History, American History, Civics (also called Government), and maybe Economics. There is no preferred order, so you can plug them into your plan wherever they will fit. The only consideration might be the difficulty level of the curriculum you choose.

For some reason I've always considered Civics and Economics to be senior courses (they are each only a semester), so that is when my kids have done them. But they can really happen any year.

If your child is not a history fan, you probably don't need to do any more history than this. If they love history, then additional history courses could fill in some of those elective spots on the plan.

English

English (also known as Language Arts) gets a little more complicated. Most colleges do require a full four years of high school English, so there are lots of boxes to fill on the plan. Many colleges require some type of literature course, either British literature or American literature -- or both. Beyond that it's up to you. It can be difficult to narrow down from the vast selection of possibilities.

I went the simple route (you should have figured out by now that that is my standard M.O., lol) and did two more years of grammar in 9th and 10th grade, and then two years of literature in 11th and 12th. There are lots of resources for high school English out there. For now just fill in your plan with general course names (e.g., American Literature); as you research curriculum, you can get more specific.

Foreign Language

Not everyone considers foreign language to be a core course; some call it an elective. It's really personal preference, but I call it a core course because most colleges do require at least two credits of a foreign language. They also usually expect both years to be the same language, to show that the student studied it in some depth.

This again is an easy thing to plug into your plan. Just choose the language your child wants to learn and find two spots for it on your plan. Spanish 1 and Spanish 2, for example. Easy-peasy. No need to add a third or fourth year unless it's something your child is interested in; it is harder to find curriculum for the advanced levels.

The Next Step?

First, if you haven't done so already, be sure to finish filling in the specific core courses you want for your child in the appropriate blanks in the *Planning Core Courses* chart. Again, just names of courses; we're not picking curriculum yet.

Also print out the High School Coursework chart (yes, there isa second printable for this chapter!) and transfer the results of your work from the *Planning Core Courses* chart onto there.

You might notice, especially if your child will not be taking math, science, or history for all four years, that there are a lot of empty spots in the plan for junior and senior years. That's where electives come in. Those are next, so if you've completed the plan thus far, turn the page to keep going!

Planning Core Courses

	Grade 8	Grade 9	Grade 10
English/Language Arts			
Math			
History/Social Studies			
Science			
Foreign Language			

	Grade 11	Grade 12	NOTES
English/Language Arts			
Math			
History/Social Studies			
Science			
Foreign Language			

High School Coursework

Grade 8/9			Grade 10		
Subject	**Course**	**Credits**	**Subject**	**Course**	**Credits**
	Total			**Total**	

Grade 11			Grade 12		
Subject	**Course**	**Credits**	**Subject**	**Course**	**Credits**
	Total			**Total**	

Chapter Six

Planning Electives

Planning for your teen's high school electives is the funnest part of the whole process of high school curriculum planning! Here you can get creative and enjoy the process of exploring your child's interests. One of the beauties of homeschooling high school is that those interests don't have to take extra time in addition to school; they can be an integral part of school. Which means a more relaxed day for the whole family! Happiness!

I don't actually try to get specific about high school electives until just prior to each year or semester. My kids' interests seem to change with the weather, lol. I want electives to be fun for them, a chance to explore something that they enjoy in further detail. There is always the danger that having to do schoolwork for a particular topic will take the fun out of it, but that is a chance we take. If they still like it after taking it as a course, that may mean it's a possible career path!

So for this part of our planning, we are just going to make a list of possibilities for our teen. Or teens, if you have more than one starting high school within the next year or two. First I'll give some general information about electives; then I'll provide a list of some of the possibilities that we used in our own homeschool. There are lotsa articles out there with more ideas, too.

Go ahead and print out the *Electives Brainstorming List* from the end of the chapter. As you read through those I've listed, jot down the ones that might be interesting or helpful for your child.

General Information about Electives

Some courses that I used as electives were actually in core subject areas such as science and language arts. But if the student had already completed high school core requirements in that subject area, then I counted the extra course as an elective.

Not all high school electives have to be for a letter grade.

There are several that I put on their transcript as pass/fail courses. I do that mostly because I don't think Driver's Ed, for example, is worth giving a full-fledged A to, thus skewing the GPA in a positive direction. Nor do I want to give written tests for it, so as to feel like an A was earned -- I just want to give credit for the time spent learning to drive. Counting that the same as earning an A in history or math seems unfair to me.

Prepping for standardized tests was another P/F course in our house (they put in the hours, but I didn't expect them to prove learning to me), as was Early Childhood Education (one daughter spent a lot of hours nanny-ing for a local family).

The flip side of that coin is that you don't want to have too many P/F courses on the transcript. So some electives will definitely need to be ones that you feel comfortable giving a letter grade to, because the course requires a reasonable amount of work and learning.

Examples of this type of elective would be an extra science course such as Astronomy, or something your child is focusing on as a possible career path like serious art or music study. In these types of courses there is evaluation of learning such as tests, papers, portfolios, recitals, etc.

When considering how much credit to give for high school electives, the following rule of thumb is a good one: **a .5-credit course should encompass at least 60 hours of work. Thus 1 credit would be a minimum of 120 hours of work.** This is not necessarily true for core courses -- for them, more hours is a good idea (more like 150-180). But for electives, the requirements need not be so stringent.*

For the P/F type of elective, logging hours is a great way to prove that the credit is deserved. Once the child has reached 60 hours, you can give them 1/2 a credit. A true confession would be that I also occasionally used the TLAR method: That Looks About Right. I didn't log every time I gave my child driving instruction; but I do know that over time it came to at least 60 hours. (And probably took at least that much off my life span…) Especially if you count the time they took reading and studying the book to prepare for the written exams at the licensing office.

Here's another crazy thought: not all the time for a course has to take place in the semester you place it on the transcript.

Driver's ed is a great example for this idea, too. All of my kids took over a year from start to finish for the driver's ed process. I placed the course on their transcript for the semester in which they finished.

We get so wrapped up in how high school is "supposed" to be. We forget that WE are the decision-makers when it comes to our homeschool. We have a lot of freedom when it comes to electives, just as in every other aspect of homeschooling high school.

This is a good time to note that there is discussion among the ranks about whether to count things for credit or count them as extra-curriculars. Many people claim that extra-curriculars are important on a college application, so you don't want to count everything for credit.

If you're concerned about this, do some research -- look at those college admissions pages again and see if they list extra-curriculars as an important factor for acceptance. To be brutally honest, I don't think many are even going to mention it. But don't take my word for it -- or the word of that other person who says they're necessary. Now you know how to look things up for yourself; so do it and find out the facts.

My personal view is that it doesn't have to be an issue to stress over. I counted as much as was needed to obtain a reasonable amount of graduation credits, and whatever was left became extra-curricular (which wasn't much, btw). And no college turned my kids away for not being well-rounded individuals.

Electives We Have Done

Be aware that not all of these were used for every child, lol. Each kid is different, as I'm sure you know. I did keep our core course curriculum the same for every one of them (until we started with Classical Conversations, that is), but high school electives were based on personal interests and learning styles.

NOTE: I am giving curriculum information here for your convenience, but **don't stress about picking your own curriculum yet**. Right now is only about getting ideas for possible electives; we'll deal with curriculum selection in the next chapter.

Violin: One daughter decided in her sophomore year of high school to pursue this for a college major. So she upped her practice time to 3+ hours a day. Guess who got two credits for violin each year after that? And since she received instruction from an outside teacher who could evaluate her progress, and was required to learn theory and give recitals as evidence of learning, she received a letter grade.

Art: This was a P/F course because I do not feel competent to judge whether art is good or not. We used this curriculum and loved it: Artistic Pursuits Books 1 & 2. I have a short review on the blog.

Marine Biology: This is an example of a science course that was used as an elective. We used Apologia's Exploring Creation with Marine Biology.

Astronomy: This was a fun, hands-on course, requiring the student to observe the night sky and make maps of it, among other creative projects. We used this resource: Signs & Seasons: Understanding the Elements of Classical Astronomy.

Meteorology: We used an online course from BYU. Their

courses are actually reasonably priced and quite well done. I ignored their requirement to take a proctored final at an "official" location and just computed the final grade based on online tests and quizzes. I didn't want or need their accredited credit, lol. I can decide what is worth credit in my own homeschool. We have the pow-ah, y'all!!

Driver's Ed: We kept a loose record of hours behind the wheel and gave a P/F grade. There was also a booklet and video available from our insurance guy that one daughter was required to absorb. Oh yea, and our special driver's education field trip to the junk yard. Muahahaha...

Home Ec: One course was "Cooking" for the daughter who made dinner once a week for over a year; "Early Childhood Development" was earned for LOTS of babysitting. These were P/F.

Bible: A P/F credit given for personal and family Bible time (you could probably also include church attendance). I only used this once, but you could conceivably count it each year.

Standardized Test Prep: I detail this course in the post called Homeschool ACT and SAT Practice.

Extra foreign language: One daughter was very interested in foreign languages and wanted to learn more than just one. She ended up with a credit for Russian 1 and another for German 1 on her transcript, in addition to 4 credits of French. The French was considered a core course; but the other two I considered to be electives, so I was less stringent in the requirements for them. She did receive letter grades for them, though, because they weren't just time put in; there was evaluation of learning. Here's what we used:

French (it wasn't an elective but I'm including this info for the curious): Breaking the Barrier French -- their three books are worth 4 credits. I called and spoke to the writers themselves to verify this. *smugness*
Russian: We used another BYU online course for this. See link and further info under Meteorology above.
German: I cannot recommend the online German at Oklahoma State University enough. See a more detailed review on the blog.

PE: One daughter played softball in the local recreational league. The time she spent at practices and games was worth .5 credit each year.

Geography: Not all courses should be rigorous, or we would all get burnt out very quickly. Geography can be a way to check the elective box with a fairly easy workload, depending on the curriculum you choose. We used PAC World Geography, which is a series of workbooks similar to Lifepac.

Intro to Fiction Writing: My one daughter was interested in Creative Writing as a possible major. So this extra Language Arts course was taken as an elective, for her to get her feet wet. We used the book Learn to Write the Novel Way, which takes the student step-by-step through the process of writing a novel. Really neat!

Work-Study: My son is working 16+ hours a week at a "real" job, lol. There is no reason not to count his time as credit for school. Think of all the things he's learning about customer service, work ethic, employee relations, business practices, etc. I will probably not count it for more than 2 credits per year, however.

For more ideas for high school electives, I've created a Pinterest board where I am pinning new stuff often! Go to the resource page to follow the link, and then click on FOLLOW: Annie & Everything High School Elective Ideas Pinterest Board

For now, try to solidify which electives your teen will take during their ninth grade year. Each year (or each semester, lol), you can come back and make final selections for the next one. Notate the ninth-grade electives on the *High School Coursework* chart. You can pencil in some possibilities for the other years, if you like. Or you can just write "elective," knowing you will fill in the details later.

Once you've gotten as far as planning high school electives, you've gotten to the easy part! Whether you are giving a letter grade or it's just a pass/fail course, your kids will enjoy doing something other than the hardcore subjects for part of their day. And here is where flexibility and creativity can come into play, as you work with each child to develop a wonderful homeschool high school experience for both of you. Woot!!

*http://www.hslda.org/highschool/docs/EvaluatingCredits.asp

Electives Brainstorming

Name	Credits	Name	Credits

Name	Credits	Name	Credits

Chapter Seven

Choosing the Best Curriculum for YOUR Homeschool

Have you ever heard the phrase "there's more than one way to skin a cat"? Um, there probably really is, although let's not dwell on that thought. My point right now is that the same is true about the process of getting knowledge into your teen's head. There are LOTSA ways to do it! LOL. AP, online, dual enrollment, textbook, unit studies, hands-on, honors, remedial, workbook, research paper, recitation, co-op, apprenticeship, etc. etc. etc.!

Please allow me to reassure you once again that your choices about these -- whatever route you decide to go -- should be about what works for YOUR family. Not about what so-and-so said they think is necessary. You now know what you need to do to meet the requirements for your child's goals, whether they involve college or not, and you don't need to bow to the pressure of trying to match someone else's ideas.

Let me also say that if your family's needs mean that your child will not be doing any type of schooling outside the home -- no dual enrollment, no co-op, no online classes -- that is also perfectly fine. Many times that is either a logistical issue or a budgetary issue; for our family, it was both, lol.

Our kids did high school mostly from curriculum that I could purchase and bring into the house. That meant a lot of text-books and workbooks, with the occasional online class (but only the most inexpensive ones I could find, and only when I couldn't find a standard curriculum that would teach the content well). My kids have not taken a single dual enrollment class. Guess what? They also have not done any AP or honors courses. And it did NOT affect their ability to get into the colleges they applied to.

So if you are overwhelmed by the thought of driving your kid to a dual enrollment class three times a week, or if you can't afford anything online, or if you don't like the thought of the extra work involved in an AP or honors course -- don't even worry about it! And don't be intimidated when others talk about these things. You are not ruining your kid's chances or limiting his opportunities. I know this from my own experience.

(Speaking of experience, have you ever noticed that most often the people saying these things haven't even had a kid apply to college yet? Or maybe they've had one -- and that one was a brainiac. Remember to consider the source when you hear this type of intimidation. Just sayin'.)

One more piece of encouragement I want to give to you: do not be afraid of higher level math or science.

You do NOT have to "teach" these subjects to your teen. Pick a curriculum that is designed for independent study -- then your teen can teach himself! -- or choose an online class, a co-op, or even a tutor for outside accountability and help. There are a wealth of options out there for your child to learn what they need to without your needing to know the material.

You really CAN do this homeschool high school thing -- I promise!

Now, with all that out of the way, it's time to choose specific curriculum for each of those boxes on our plan!! Woot! This is where all this thought time comes to fruition and you can select the means by which to get this plan accomplished.

Don't worry; we're not going to do all four years at once, lol. **Right now, just concentrate on the first year.** You already have a plan for the courses; that's the important part. It would be overwhelming to try to choose ALL four years of curriculum at once. You can come back to this part as many times as needed throughout the high school years.

I personally have always been a procrastinator when it comes to curriculum planning; I usually don't get started until some-time in July. I am always too caught up in the current year to want to start looking at the next one! I don't know how people can be so organized that they have it all planned out by May or June! But if you are one of them, good for you!!

This part of the process is something you have to do all by yourself, I'm afraid. I do have a handy-dandy printable for you, and some advice about where to go looking; but only you know your kids -- how they learn best -- and your plan. Only you know how you like to homeschool, whether that be with unit studies or online classes or textbooks or whatever.

And if you don't really know that stuff yet, because you're new to homeschooling, then researching all sorts of curriculum is the way to figure it out. Then you can discover what resonates with you, what your teen might work with best, what sounds workable for your family, and what does not. I suggest taking one course at a time and looking at many different curriculum possibilities until you find one that you think will work best for your situation.

In case it will help, I'll share what I look for in a curriculum.

These qualifications are what work best for our family -- and my sanity level, lol.

Not too much teacher involvement or preparation. Even in the younger years, there were only certain subjects I was willing to be very involved in -- such as math and reading. The others, I felt, could be done fairly independently. Certainly now, with kids in middle and high school, I look for curriculum that can be done almost completely by the student. In the early years I looked for independent learning curriculum because there was only so much of me to go around; now, though, it is because at this level I think they are ready to work on their own.

As easy on the budget as possible. Because of our somewhat large family, buying new curriculum each year for every student (as in consumable workbooks, for example) would be expensive. I look for curriculum that is packaged as a hardbound textbook or some other non-consumable format, so that it can be used again and again as the years go by.

Usually of a fairly challenging difficulty level. If a curriculum is known to be pretty easy, I generally avoid it. I'd rather take a challenging curriculum and have to omit parts and scale back on it than have a curriculum that is too easy that I now have to find things to supplement with. That's just too much work for me!

Gets good reviews from those that have used it. I always try to read lots of reviews for any product I am considering. Usually the user reviews will have more detailed information than the sales material from the publisher. I like to know the nuts and bolts of how a curriculum works before I decide to purchase.

I will usually look in these places to find reviews:

1 My high school Facebook group has become a GREAT place to hear how a specific curriculum has worked for people. You can use the search box at the top or start a new thread to ask for what people think of one that you are considering. Or just say "Favorite Algebra 1 curriculum?" and be prepared for LOTSA suggestions!! Go to the link: It's Not That Hard to Homeschool High School.

2 The Well-Trained Mind forum -- I use the High School and Self-Education Board frequently to search and find out what others think about a specific curriculum. Sometimes I'll ask a question myself. There is also a K-8 Curriculum Board, although I've not been on there.

3 Rainbow Resource Center -- Their catalog every year is always larger than phone book size, and it is chock full of lengthy descriptions and reviews of the products they sell. All that same information is available at their website.

4 Christian Book Distributors -- They have user reviews at the bottom of the page, after the usual write-up about a product. They might also have sample pages and/or lessons that you can download.

5 The website of the publisher or author of the curriculum -- Here, too, you might find sample pages and/or lessons. You might also be able to email or call them if you have any questions that are not answered elsewhere.

6 Cathy Duffy Reviews — Back in the day, Cathy Duffy started by writing an actual book of curriculum reviews for homeschoolers. Now, her thorough reviews and explanations for about a gazillion different products can be read online. She also does have an updated version of her book; it not only includes reviews but also information about how to determine your homeschool philosophy and your children's learning styles, and other helpful information to guide you in choosing curriculum.

I know my own curriculum planning preferences are not for everyone, but I present them here to help you determine your own. One of the beauties of homeschooling these days is that there are so many options out there, and each family can decide what works best for them! Don't ya just love that??

So now it is time to print out several copies of the *Curriculum Choice Research* printable at the end of the chapter -- and start googling! Put each subject on a different page, so you can keep all your possibilities for one subject together. If you wait until July, like me, you'll have to work fairly quickly in order to make a selection and purchase and allow for shipping time. So yea; it might be best to start a bit earlier than that so you have time to really examine all the options. This is one time where #doasIsaynotasIdo might apply, lol.

This chapter is another that has a second printable, because once you start making choices of which exact curriculum to use, you'll need a place to put it! Print out the *Course & Curriculum Schedule* form and begin to write in your final choices for curriculum. First you'll transpose the general information from the *High School Coursework* form, then specify the curriculum next to that. This form is designed for you to fit one year onto each page -- because with both full- and half-credit courses, you might need a lot of room! -- so eventually you will have 4-5 pages that reflect your child's high school career in full.

This is one time that you can proceed to the next chapter in the book, however, even if you're not done (or even started!) your curriculum research. There I will hit some big picture things to think about when it comes to whether or not your child will be prepared for life after high school. If you keep the ideas I mention there in mind as you choose curriculum, you'll be even more confident that you will not be ruining your child's life by schooling them at home through graduation!

But wait! There's more!

Hey, before we end this chapter, I do want to repeat ONE MORE TIME what I said earlier about whether or not you need to do. all. the. things. Except this time it will be in video form! I'm including a link to an FB Live that I made in my group one day. Please watch it to be fully convinced that however you want your child to learn is TOTALLY OK. You don't have to do more than you are comfortable with or that works for your WHOLE family. Go here: Are all of those things necessary?

Now onto the next chapter, for even more encouragement as you prepare for your teen's high school experience!

Curriculum Choice Research

Subject/Course _____

Title of Curriculum _____

Style _____

Reviews ☆☆☆☆☆

Pros
_____
_____
_____

Cons
_____
_____
_____

Places to Buy	Price	Shipping	Total

Title of Curriculum _____

Style _____

Reviews ☆☆☆☆☆

Pros
_____
_____
_____

Cons
_____
_____
_____

Places to Buy	Price	Shipping	Total

Final Course & Curriculum Schedule

Grade _____

Subject	Course Name	Curriculum	Credits
		Total	

Chapter Eight

More Encouragement as You Plan

How are you feeling now?? Hopefully quite A LOT better. Once you've educated yourself and put a plan together, it's much easier to feel like you might actually know what you're doing when it comes to homeschooling high school! Yes, there will still be challenges -- any mom of a teen knows this -- but now that you've been through the process of research and decision-making once, it will be easier to do it again when you need to fine-tune anything.

And yet you might have some lingering fears.

Just because you've made a plan and chosen some of your child's curriculum, you might still be feeling like there is no guarantee that they will be ready for college or "real" life.

And you'd be right. Academics alone do not make a person capable of succeeding at being a responsible person or meeting the demands of college life. It would be silly to rely solely on our *Course & Curriculum Schedule* for that.

So let's look at the bigger picture for a minute -- because I think that will help you see how everything you're doing as a homeschool mom truly WILL prepare your teen for the world that lies ahead, in whatever direction they may take. Much of what is needed comes naturally to the average, conscientious homeschool parent (which you are, if you are taking the time to read this). In fact, you are probably doing some of these already, even if you've gotten no higher than middle school with your child so far.

If you do these things, then you can be confident that you are giving your teen adequate preparation for most of adult life:

1 Teach your teen to learn independently. This will probably have been started in middle school (or earlier!), but if not, now is the time. What this means is guiding your teen to take ownership of learning the content of their courses. In other words, the high school student should be reading the lesson or watching the video and then completing the assignment without relying on you for instruction or explanation. They should be checking their daily work and learning from their mistakes. They should be studying for tests on their own. Your involvement should only be to answer the occasional question and to grade tests and papers.

Why is this so important? Because that is what college is. In college your child is given a syllabus and is expected to follow it. He is expected to stay on track with assignments and turn papers in on time. He is expected to seek out help when he doesn't understand; no one will hold his hand and check in on him.

And in the working world, it is important to be able to learn new skills easily. A boss will appreciate an employee who is capable of reading instructions and following them well.

And let's just talk about life in general: don't you want your child to be able to change directions later if they need or want to? The ability to learn new things for themselves will mean they never stagnate or feel stuck. They will have the capacity to develop an entirely new skill set -- or even just start a new hobby!

If your teen is in charge of most of their learning while they are in high school and being generally successful, then you can feel certain they are being well prepared for college and adulthood.

2 Give them a strong language arts foundation. In my opinion, language arts is more important than science or math. Because if the child has good grammar and a wide vocabulary, understands how to read higher level subject matter, and can express himself through speech and writing, then he will be able to read and understand just about anything that is thrown at him in college or on the job, including the science and math.

The reverse -- that the child who can handle high level math will be able to read and understand other subjects -- may not be true. All college majors and jobs involve using language; not all of them involve math and science. So don't give up on the grammar just because they are in high school. Encourage reading of all genres. Give them lots of opportunities to write. If your teen is capable of handling the English language well, then you can be confident they will be ready to tackle college coursework or their new career.

3 Teach them to manage their time. This is related to #1 but isn't exactly the same. Sometimes a kid is able to learn independently just fine, but they don't discipline themselves to do it in a timely fashion. In college they will need to juggle classes, work, sleep, and their burgeoning social life. As a working adult, it's not much different. Give them opportunities to practice now. Give them opportunities to fail now. It's definitely better for them to suffer consequences and learn lessons in time management now at home rather than later at college, when you are spending the big bucks! Or on the job, when it could mean dismissal. If you are teaching your teen to be responsible for how they use their time, then you are doing a good job of preparing them for life.

(4) Don't always let them redo everything to get an A. This is one of my pet peeves with homeschoolers. Of course we want mastery, but if we always let the kid retake every test or rewrite every paper, they never learn to do it right the first time.

I gave my kids B's (and lower) when they deserved them. I think a transcript with all A's is suspect. Yes, there are plenty of kids who earn them -- but do they earn all A's, or might there be an A- or two in there? Or even -- gasp! -- a B+? Every homeschooled kid is not an A student, y'all. Don't try to pretend they are, just because you would like them to be. They won't get the opportunity to redo things in college or at work. If you are holding your teen accountable for the quality of their work the FIRST time, then you can know that they won't be overwhelmed by the same expectation elsewhere.

With college prep specifically, though, there are other factors that will help you feel affirmed about whether you are doing an adequate job:

 The SAT and ACT are good indicators of whether your child is ready for college. If the scores from these tests are rather low, you might want to consider some other type of career path. If the scores are average or above average, then your child has the ability to handle college-level work. This is completely objective, y'all. No homeschool mom bias here.

2 Colleges are aware that freshmen need help adjusting to college-level work and college-level expectations. Often there is an entire course during the very first semester that teaches the freshmen about study skills, time management, how to use the library, etc.

There is usually also a huge support system for freshmen, from the RA on their dorm floor, to orientation small groups, to student mentors, and more. Many college professors who teach freshmen classes are more communicative when it comes to expectations and scheduling, as well as giving lots of feedback on assignments. Knowing this on the front end can help allay fears about your child being able to adapt. They are given every opportunity during that first year to learn everything they need to know.

3 And then there's the consideration of what type of college you are trying to prepare your child for anyway. Sometimes I think we homeschoolers feel like we have to plan as if our child will be going to an Ivy League school, because if we shoot for anything less, we're not measuring up to the "homeschool elite" out there who have been winning the national spelling bees and acing the honors courses and running their own businesses by age 18. Guess what? Most of us are ordinary. Most of us will be sending our children to the local community college or state school, or maybe a small private school. Those places will LOVE your homeschooled child. Or at the very least, they won't expect them to be a superstar of the highest order. It's OK to have an average student going to an average college, y'all!!

4 THERE IS HELP. You are not in this alone! Check out my High School Homeschool Blogroll for a list of blogs that regularly write about homeschooling high school. Lotsa great information there.

Then there's my Facebook group, It's Not that Hard to Homeschool High School, where you can ask any question you want and get wonderful feedback from many moms who have felt just like you. When you have support, it is SOOOO much easier to be confident in what you are doing!

I know how insecure we can feel when thinking about homeschooling high school, especially when it comes to preparation for the big, bad world. But I'm here to say that you've got this!! By paying attention to the things I've listed above, you can be confident that you're giving your teen everything they need to be successful. Remember, this is all coming from a mom who has graduated three who all got accepted to college and didn't flunk out after they got there. :-)

So no more worries, OK??

Now What?

So, this has been a bit of a journey, hasn't it? But now you have a handful of documents that comprise your plan for high school, AND you've developed a new mindset about what it means to homeschool your teen all the way through to graduation.

Does it look different now than you thought it would? Hopefully in a good way. A doable way. A more confidence-inducing way. :-)

As you move forward, keep referring to your plan.

Like when you get afraid because of something someone else has said -- pull your plan out and remind yourself of why you set it up the way you did. Remember the research and knowledge that went into it.

Or when something isn't working well. It might be just the need for a change in curriculum, but it might also mean the plan needs to be re-evaluated. No big deal; when you know why you planned the way you did in the first place, it is easier to pinpoint what needs to be fixed -- and how to make it better.

With each new teen that enters high school, you may want to start back at the beginning again. In our family, we had a new set of graduation requirements for each one. Because they are all different, aren't they? Requiring my artist

#2 daughter to do the same amount of math as the first would have ended in frustration for all concerned, lol. The second time through the process will go faster, trust me.

And every year, you can pull out the *Curriculum Choice Review* forms and start looking for curriculum to fulfill the plan for that year. It's good to do this fresh every year, as you discover more about how your child learns best and what they're drawn to. I love leaving electives blank until the last minute for that very reason -- a teen's interests change with the tide, don't they?

Keep on marching, homeschool mom.

You CAN do this homeschool high school thing!! With a plan in hand that is based on solid research of actual facts, you have everything you need to have a successful high school experience with your teen! I have confidence in you!!

Thanks so much for purchasing and reading this book. Feel free to let me know if you have any questions or concerns about what I've written, or if I've not addressed something that you feel I should have. If you've been helped, feel free to let me know that, too. :-)

Hugs!!

-- Ann

About the Author

Ann Karako is the (very) middle-aged mom of five who writes at Annie & Everything about calming the chaos of homeschool life. She says, "I don't do complicated!" and is known for her down-to-earth common sense about all things homeschool and the homeschool lifestyle.

Having graduated three children (the fourth within a month of this writing, with one more to go after that), she has a heart for helping families choose to homeschool all the way through high school.

She admins the popular FB group called It's Not that Hard to Homeschool High School as a place of encouragement and support for moms of homeschooled teens. She and her family, including two dogs and three cats, live in rural Missouri.

You can also find her on Facebook and Pinterest.

College Requirements Cross-section

	College #1	College #2
Name of School		
Math		
Number of Credits		
Specific Required Courses		
Unacceptable Courses		
English/Language Arts		
Number of Credits		
Specific Required Courses		
Unacceptable Courses		
History/Social Studies		
Number of Credits		
Specific Required Courses		
Unacceptable Courses		
Science		
Number of Credits		
Number of Lab Courses		
Specific Required Courses		
Unacceptable Courses		
Fine Arts		
Number of Credits		
Specific Required Courses		
Unacceptable Courses		
Foreign Language		
Number of Credits		
Specific Required Courses		
Unacceptable Courses		
Electives		
Number of Credits		
Specific Required Courses		
Unacceptable Courses		

Graduation Requirements Planning

Directions: Fill out the column under Trial #1 first with possible numbers of required credits in each subject row.
Then try a new scenario in the Trial #2 column, and so on.

	Trial #1	Trial #2	Trial #3	Trial #4	Trial #5
English/Language Arts					
Math					
History/Social Studies					
Science					
Foreign Language					
Fine Arts					
Electives					
_____					
_____					
_____					
Total					

General Credits Plan

Directions: Write the number of credits for each subject in the box under the appropriate grade.

	Grade 8	Grade 9	Grade 10	Grade 11	Grade 12
English/Language Arts					
Math					
History/Social Studies					
Science					
Foreign Language					
Fine Arts					
Electives					
_____					
_____					
_____					
Total:					

Planning Core Courses

	Grade 8	Grade 9	Grade 10
English/Language Arts			
Math			
History/Social Studies			
Science			
Foreign Language			

	Grade 11	Grade 12	NOTES
English/Language Arts			
Math			
History/Social Studies			
Science			
Foreign Language			

High School Coursework

Grade 8/9			Grade 10		
Subject	**Course**	**Credits**	**Subject**	**Course**	**Credits**
		Total			Total

Grade 11			Grade 12		
Subject	**Course**	**Credits**	**Subject**	**Course**	**Credits**
		Total			Total

Electives Brainstorming

Name	Credits	Name	Credits

Name	Credits	Name	Credits

Curriculum Choice Research

Subject/Course _____

Title of Curriculum _____

Style _____

Reviews ☆☆☆☆☆

Pros
_____
_____
_____

Cons
_____
_____
_____

Places to Buy	Price	Shipping	Total

Title of Curriculum _____

Style _____

Reviews ☆☆☆☆☆

Pros
_____
_____
_____

Cons
_____
_____
_____

Places to Buy	Price	Shipping	Total

Final Course & Curriculum Schedule

Grade _____

Subject	Course Name	Curriculum	Credits
			Total

Made in United States
Orlando, FL
17 December 2023

41232415R00049